Collins

easy le

Counting
workbook

Ages
3–5

Carol Medcalf

How to use this book

- Find a quiet, comfortable place to work, away from distractions.
- This book has been written in a logical order, so start at the first page and work your way through.
- Try to use the following language as you work through the book together: add, plus, take away, minus, more than, less than, equals, all together, left over, set/s, half.
- Help with reading the instructions where necessary and ensure that your child understands what to do.
- When questions have two parts, it is often best to gain the first answer and record it before moving on to the next part of the question.
- If an activity is too difficult for your child then do more of our suggested practical activities (see Parent's tip) and return to the page when you know that they're likely to achieve it.
- Some children find it easier if all the other activities on the page are covered with a blank piece of paper, so only the activity they are working on is visible.
- Always end each activity before your child gets tired so that they will be eager to return next time.
- Help and encourage your child to check their own answers as they complete each activity.
- Let your child return to their favourite pages once they have been completed. Talk about the activities they enjoyed and what they have learnt.

Special features of this book:

- **Parent's tip:** situated at the bottom of every left-hand page, this suggests further activities and encourages discussion about what your child has learnt.
- **Progress panel:** situated at the bottom of every right-hand page, the number of animals and stars shows your child how far they have progressed through the book. Once they have completed each double page, ask them to colour in the white star.
- **Certificate:** the certificate on the inside back cover should be used to reward your child for their effort and achievement. Remember to give them plenty of praise and encouragement, regardless of how they do.

Published by Collins
An imprint of HarperCollins*Publishers* Ltd
The News Building
1 London Bridge Street
London
SE1 9GF

Browse the complete Collins catalogue at collins.co.uk

© HarperCollins*Publishers* Ltd 2013
This edition © HarperCollins*Publishers* Ltd 2015

10 9

ISBN 978-0-00-815228-4

The author asserts the moral right to be identified as the author of this work.

All rights reserved. No part of this publication may be reproduced, stored in a retrieval system, or transmitted, in any form or by any means, electronic, mechanical, photocopying, recording or otherwise, without the prior permission of Collins.

British Library Cataloguing in Publication Data

A Catalogue record for this publication is available from the British Library

Written by Carol Medcalf
Page layout by Linda Miles, Lodestone Publishing and Contentra Technologies Ltd
Illustrated by Jenny Tulip
Cover design by Sarah Duxbury and Paul Oates
Cover illustration by John Haslam
Project managed by Chantal Peacock and Sonia Dawkins

Printed in Great Britain by Bell and Bain Ltd.

MIX
Paper from responsible source
FSC™ C007454

This book is produced from independently certified FSC™ paper to ensure responsible forest management.

For more information visit:
www.harpercollins.co.uk/green

Contents

Numbers 0–10

● Join the dots to write the numbers. Count and colour the counters.

Label cupcake cases from 0–5 and ask your child to place the correct number of small objects, such as beads, into each cupcake case. Slowly increase the number of cupcake cases as your child gets better at the activity.

Numbers 11–20

● Join the dots to write the numbers. Count and colour the counters.

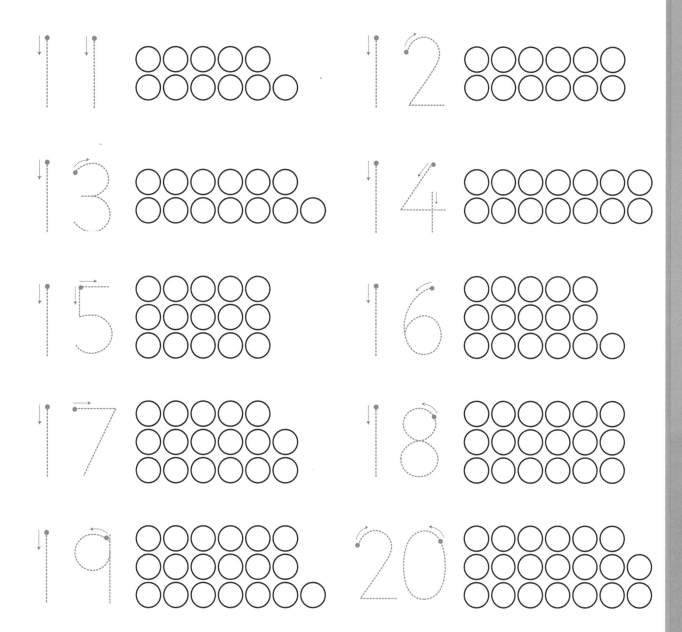

Well done!
Now colour
the star.

Counting to 10

● Count the animals in each circle and draw a line to match the circle to the right number.

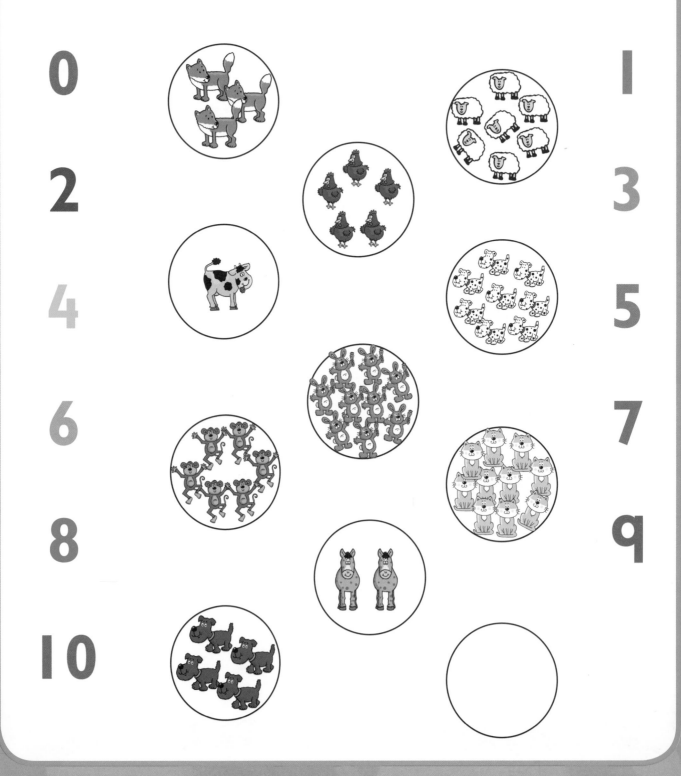

0

2

4

6

8

10

1

3

5

7

q

Use cards containing numbers from 0 to 20 and some objects placed into piles. Ask your child to match the number cards with the piles of objects by counting, like in this activity. Start with low numbers and slowly increase the numbers and piles of objects.

Counting to 20

● Count the objects in each circle and draw a line to match the circle to the right number.

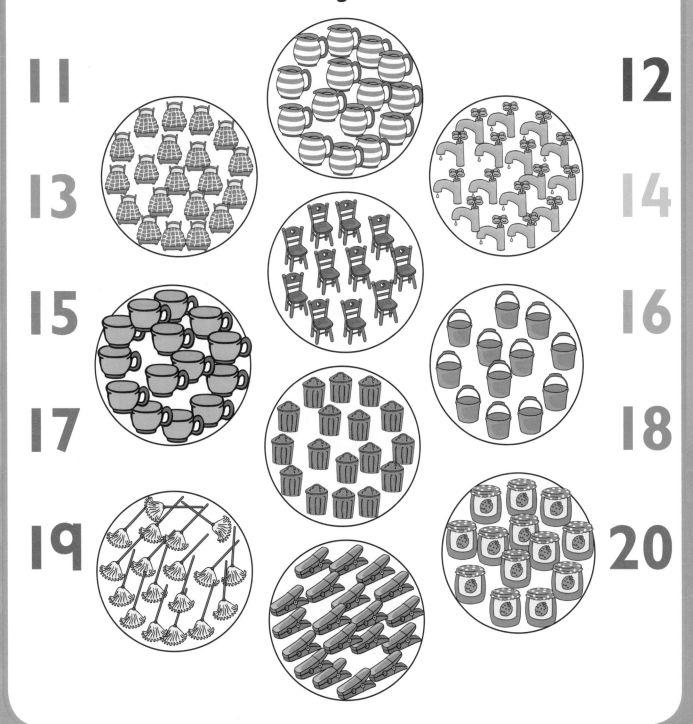

11

12

13

14

15

16

17

18

19

20

Number practice

- How many spots does each snake have?
  Circle the snake that has the most.
  Tick the snake that has the least.
  Join the two together that have the same.

- Can you draw the right number of spots on the snakes?

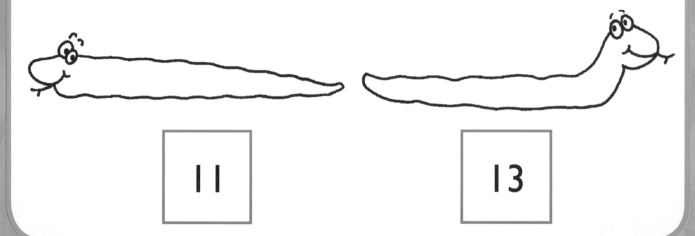

11

13

Odd one out

● Look at the pictures in each row and circle the odd one out.

● Circle the odd number out in each row.

6 6 6 6 9 6 6 6 6 6

7 1 7 7 7 7 7 7 7 7

3 3 3 3 3 3 3 8 3 3

5 5 5 5 5 4 5 5 5 5

Well done!
Now colour
the next star.

More, less and same

● How many children are in each group? Write the numbers below and circle the end of the seesaw that has more children.

● Which dog has less food? Draw more food so that the brown dog has more than the spotty dog.

● Draw a line to match the rabbits that have the same number of carrots.

- Count the towers below and write the number next to each one.
  - Colour the tower with the most bricks red.
  - Colour the tower with the least bricks blue.
  - Colour the two that are the same green.

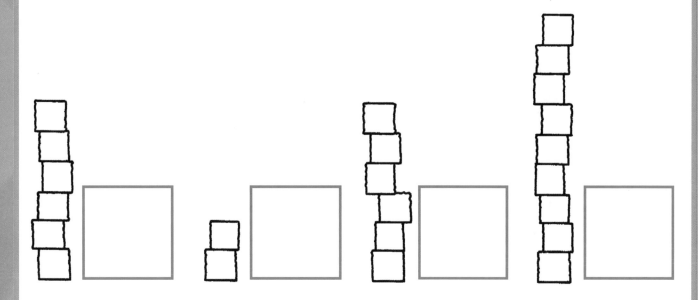

- Count the bricks and write the number in the boxes, then draw two bigger towers of your own.

Number patterns

● What pattern comes next in each row?

● Finish the number patterns.

1 2 3 1 ___ ___   2 3 4 2 ___ ___

3 4 5 3 ___ ___   9 10 9 10 ___ ___

● Can you make your own patterns here?

___ ___ ___ ___ ___ ___ ___ ___

___ ___ ___ ___ ___ ___ ___ ___

Number order

These children are muddled up. Can you write their numbers in the right order?

Can you write the kite numbers in the right order?

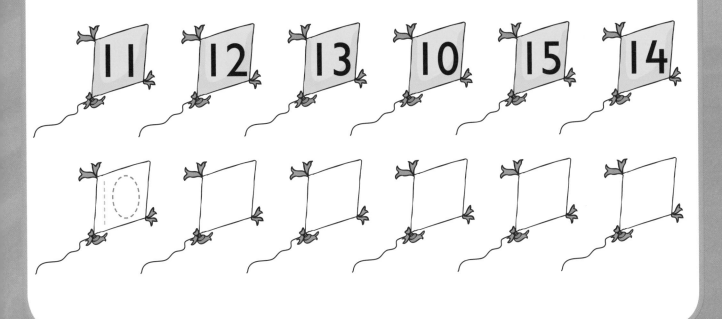

Well done! Now colour the next star.

Sets

- Look at these pictures.
  How many frogs are on the lily pad?
  How many frogs are in the water?

How many fish are in the net?
How many fish got away?

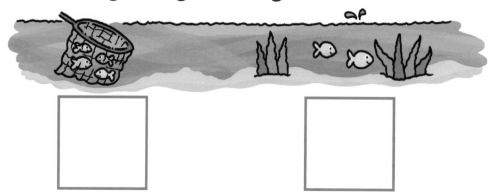

How many birds are in the nest?
How many are flying away?

Make your own sets using string or rope and put real objects in sets. This is a lot of fun when using real objects and easier to understand. Count how many objects are in each set, how many are out of the set. Make them as easy or complicated as you like to suit your child.

● Count and write how many objects are in each set.

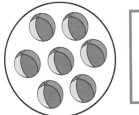 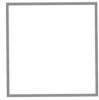 [ ]

  [ ]

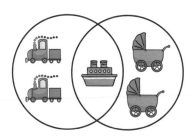

How many toys altogether? [ ]

How many toys altogether? [ ]

● Now look at these sets.

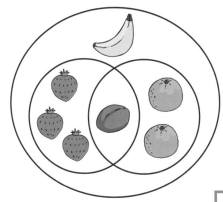

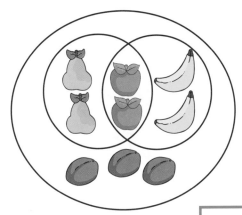

How many fruits altogether?

How many fruits altogether?

Well done! Now colour the next star.

15

Add up to 5

- Draw the answers to these sums.

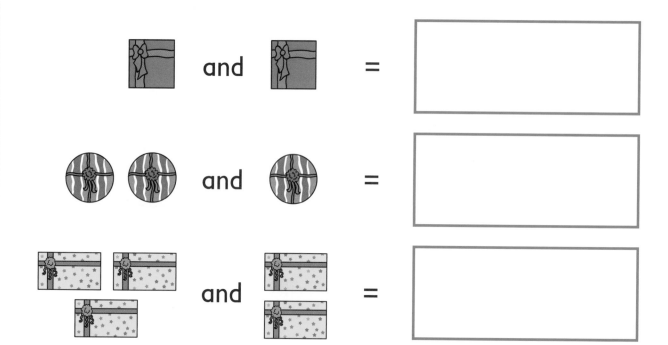

and =

and =

and =

- '+' is the sign we use when we need to add numbers together. Look at the sums below.

How many fish altogether?

=

How many birds altogether?

=

Dominoes or games using two dice are great for simple adding. Count the dots on each domino together. Add more dominoes or dice to make it harder.

● How many fingers altogether? Add these sums.

+   =   [   ]

+   =   [   ]

+   =   [   ]

+   =   [   ]

● Can you add these sums and write the answers in the boxes? Count the numbers on your fingers.

3 + 1 = [   ]   3 + 2 = [   ]

4 + 1 = [   ]   1 + 1 = [   ]

5 + 0 = [   ]   2 + 1 = [   ]

Well done!
Now colour
the next star.

Take away to 5

- '−' is the sign we use when we need to take numbers away from each other.
  Look at the apples on the tree. The wind blew and 1 apple fell off. Count how many apples are left on the tree.

How many? _____ _____ left

The sum looks like this 4 − 1 = 3

- Complete the following sums.

5 − 1 =

5 − 5 =

- Cross out the amount of the second number in the first picture to find the answer.

Cross out 1 cake in the first picture to find the answer.

$$3 \quad - \quad 1 \quad = \quad \boxed{}$$

Cross out 2 sweets in the first picture to find the answer.

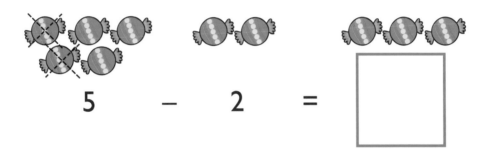

$$5 \quad - \quad 2 \quad = \quad \boxed{}$$

Cross out 2 lollies in the first picture to find the answer.

$$4 \quad - \quad 2 \quad = \quad \boxed{}$$

Well done! Now colour the next star.

Add up to 10

Always look carefully at the sign in the sum to see what to do. These sums use the **add** or **plus** sign '+'.

● Can you add these sums?

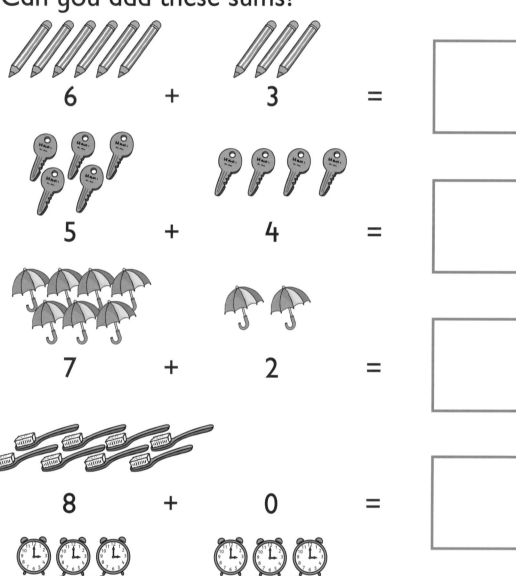

6   +   3   =   ☐

5   +   4   =   ☐

7   +   2   =   ☐

8   +   0   =   ☐

5   +   5   =   ☐

Take away to 10

Look carefully at the sign to see what to do. These sums use the **take away** or **minus** sign '–'.

● Can you take away these sums?

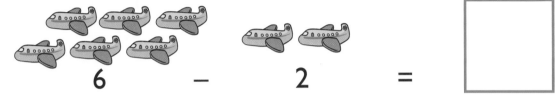

6   –   2   =   ☐

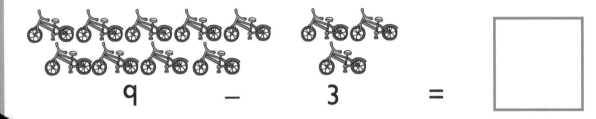

9   –   3   =   ☐

7   –   1   =   ☐

10   –   5   =   ☐

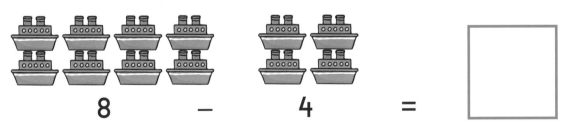

8   –   4   =   ☐

Well done!
Now colour
the next star.

You can do it

Now you can count, add and take away.

When you count, count slowly. Using your finger to point often helps.

When you see this sign '+', 'plus' or 'add', you join numbers together.

● Can you add these sums?

+ = ☐   + = ☐

+ = ☐   + = ☐

● The '+' sign in these sums is missing. Can you write them in?

3 + 6 = 9   7   3 = 10

5   3 = 8   8   2 = 10

Use all the different words for add and take away so it will become natural for your child to hear 'plus', 'add', 'increase', 'minus', 'take away', 'subtract', 'decrease'.

When you see this sign '−', 'take away' or 'minus', you take numbers away.

- Can you take away these sums?
Remember to cross some beads out in the first picture. The first two have been done to help you.

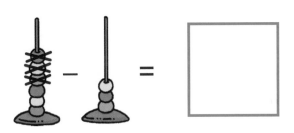

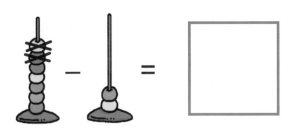

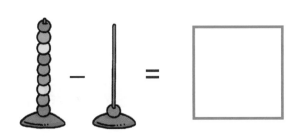

he '−' sign in these sums is missing. Can you write hem in?

7 −−−−− 3 = 4   10   5 = 5

9   1 = 8   10   10 = 0

Well done!
Now colour
the next star.

Answers

Page 4
Child to join dots and colour the counters

Page 5
Child to join dots and colour the counters

Page 6
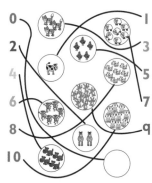
0 1 2 3 4 5 6 7 8 9 10

Page 7
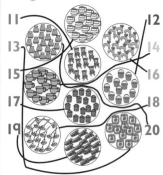
11 12 13 14 15 16 17 18 19 20

Page 8

| 6 | 6 | 12 |

| 15 | 9 | 14 |

Child's own completed snakes

Page 9

6 6 6 6 ⑨ 6 6 6 6 6
7 ① 7 7 7 7 7 7 7 7
3 3 3 3 3 3 3 ⑧ 3 3
5 5 5 5 5 ④ 5 5 5 5

Page 10

| 4 | 2 | 2 | 1 |

Child's own completed bowl of food

Page 11
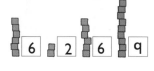

| 6 | 2 | 6 | 9 |

 | 2 | | 3 |

Child's own towers

Page 12

1 2 3 1 2 3
2 3 4 2 3 4
3 4 5 3 4 5
9 10 9 10 9 10

Child's own number patterns

Page 13
| 0 | 1 | 2 | 3 | 4 | 5 |

10 11 12 13 14 15

Page 14
3	3
4	2
2	4

Page 15
 | 7 | | 5 |

 | 5 | | 6 |

 | 7 | | 9 |

Page 16
Child's own drawing of the answers

| 5 |

| 4 |

Page 17
| 4 |

| 2 |

| 5 |

| 5 |

3 + 1 = 4   3 + 2 = 5
4 + 1 = 5   1 + 1 = 2
5 + 0 = 5   2 + 1 = 3

Page 18

How many? __4__   __3__ left

5 − 1 = 4

5 − 5 = 0

Page 19
3 − 1 = | 2 |

5 − 2 = | 3 |

4 − 2 = | 2 |

Page 20
6 + 3 = | 9 |

5 + 4 = | 9 |

7 + 2 = | 9 |

8 + 0 = | 8 |

5 + 5 = | 10 |

Page 21
6 − 2 = | 4 |

9 − 3 = | 6 |

7 − 1 = | 6 |

10 − 5 = | 5 |

8 − 4 = | 4 |

Page 22
＋ = | 5 |

＋ = | 10 |

Child's complete sums using '+'

Page 23
− = | 6 | − =

− = | 0 | − = | 8 |

Child's completed sums using '−'